Burn

poetry on fire

Stefanie Briar

ISBN: 9798722887337

Instagram: @stefanie.briar.poetry

TikTok: @stefaniebriarpoetry

Publication Date: 4/18/2021

Second Edition: 2022

Kindle Direct Publishing

Cover Art & Design: Peppermint Lines

Illustrations: Kalyani Datta

@kalyaniidatta

"Some say the world will end in fire,

some say in ice.

From what I've tasted of desire,

I hold with those who favor fire."

-Robert Frost (Excerpt from "Fire and Ice")

For the man whose fire lives on in me.

I

f
a
l
l

h e a d l o n g
into everything that lights me on fire.

I know not of restraint;
I was born to *burn*.

This is a powerful collection of poetry and prose containing fire references, themes, imagery, and/or metaphors.

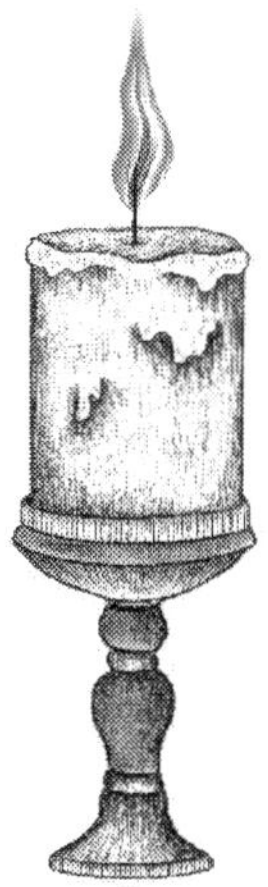

Ignite

(the self)

It hurts so beautifully,
becoming.

Life and Time:
the needle and thread.
Stitch by
s
 l
i
 p
p
 e
d
stitch,
seam by fraying seam,
you live pinprick to pinprick.

You wear the b u r n t   patina
of fading, *amnesiac* scars,
like a cloak of starlight;
like fine art under cloth.

                    -Becoming

The air was cold that night,
when I couldn't sleep and walked outside,
my feet meandering familiar earth.
Restless, I started myself a fire,
but it couldn't keep me warm.

I stared intently into the pyre,
hoping it held a message for me.
But there is no telling the future
when you've given the present up for dead,
and the past still hovers your head.

No matter the time or distance
between you and dreams come true...
when it's quiet and cold
and no one knows that you're lost,
they will not see the haunting.

No spark can ever ignite enough
to light a fire under your love
if you have already given up.

For me, my best wasn't enough
for a long, long time...

Years.

It took years of unfreezing;
of rubbing my hands for friction,
of beseeching the sun to find my face,
of allowing the warmth to sink beneath my skin.

But I did. I did it.
It was the single greatest effort
I have ever expended.

So if you're seated right now
beside metaphorical flames
but are cold to your bones...
I know. I see you.
I am here to tell you:
It is time to stand again.

You deserve nothing less than your own firepower.

Close your eyes; remember warmth.
Then, slowly, every day...choose to *b e c o m e* it.
Someday, someone may need to borrow yours.

Today, I lend you mine.

                    -Warmth

I am a human being,
not a human doing.

I can just breathe; just be.
I do not need to do everything,
to be everything,
to keep climbing,
to let ambition be the death of me.

Instead:
I will be connected.
I will be present.
I will be open to whatever lies ahead.

I will simmer and smolder; *not boil over.*

I am going to stay where I am,
learn to appreciate the view,
and take it   e a s y.

My feet will carry me on when the time comes.

There will be time enough for doing.
For now, let me *be.*

                    -Being

Loving yourself
openly,
freely,
loudly,
and without shame,
is the greatest act of rebellion
you can attach to your name.

-Rebellion

Darkness is such
a   b r i t t l e   thing.

It can be so easily defeated
by a single candle   f l i c k e r i n g.

-Candle

Patriarchy carries ancestral wounds,
bone-deep as hearts weep
thinking there will never be enough room
for all of us.

But there was, there is,
there always has been...
we've just been too busy
competing with other women to see it.

There are infinite chairs to be pulled to the table
which can keep expanding with extra leaves
for me, for you, for her,
for she who has too long remained standing.

The next time you win,
bring another woman up with you.
Lend me your hand, my sister;
I won't let go.

This is how we break cycles.
This is how our chain of love and fire grows.

                    -Hex the Patriarchy

Hell hath no fury
like a   m a d   woman
baring her teeth;
burning with the all-consuming need
to *break a glass ceiling* apart
p i e c e
                by
                    p i e c e.

-Mad Woman

I am a gypsy soul
with a   r-o-o-t-e-d   heart;

a secret garden
where art and roses b l o o m.

My passion burns,
yet my spirit *soothes*.

-Enigma

I am   r e b o r n   a bird:
comet's tail
and phoenix wings.

I do not
          fear
                 the
                     h e a d w i n d s.

                    —Fearless

There's this misconception about fire:
when it catches,
we assume we must immediately extinguish it.

We fear it.

But, when the flames finally caught me,
I stood there allowing them to incinerate me.

I felt everything heavy melt away;
everything that held me captive,
every ache and pain I carried.

When it burned itself out,
I was left in ashes,
but new.

We are all lovers of the sky;

enchanted by the watchful stars,
worshippers of the burning sun,
forever moved by the guiding moon.

Humans are just   t i d e s   that walk upright.

-Tides

Do not speak to me of strength
until you've
S
    H
      A
        D
          O
            W
         B
        O
      X
    E
D
with   f l a m e s.

         -Shadowboxer

I hold my craters
Like the surface of the
m
    o
       o
           n;
like tattoos or burn marks...
a map to the p l a c e s
that once h-e-l-d   wounds,
but now b o a s t   scars.

              -Scars

I burn my way through life.

I do not know any other way to live
but to let passion light my way,
and leave a trail of dust
in the shadows of my wake.

To the o p p r e s s e d
with no seat at the table,
dreaming of change and better days...

I will pull you up a chair
and *light f i r e s*
in your name.

-To the Oppressed

I spent my whole life trying to FIT...

into clothing two sizes too small,
into boxes never designed to   h o l d   me,
into rigid rules about *femininity*,
into a place within society dictated by *patriarchy*,
into standards of beauty I was not born holding,
into trends that felt like a *disguise*
when I tried them on for size.

So, one day,
I   q u i t.

I collected all the "does not fits"
that have plagued me all my life.

I gathered them all into a pile;
I lit them all on
F
   I
      R
         E.

                    —Standards

Unfamiliar earth can   b u r n   the soles of your feet.
First steps can *hurt,* or worse:
make you believe the chance is not worth taking.

Keep moving anyway;
stake your claim to *what you deserve.*

                    -Stake Your Claim

My force of will
could bend the center of the earth
through the eye of a needle.

I would sooner see this   w h o l e   world *burn*
than accept less than my   w o r t h.

                    -Force

I can only be held
by hands that do not fear mountains.

I can only be loved by hearts
that choose reckless abandon over fear and caution.

I can only rest my head
where my defenses can safely sleep.

I require the kind of loyalty
that would light fires and start wars.

I will be loved absolutely,
or not at all.

-Burn Notice

Stare at a nightmare for long enough,
and it starts taking the shape of comfort.

The brave stare their demons in the face
and go on living anyway.

I hope that someday

you look at all the beautiful things

that exist on this earth,

and realize one of them is **you.**

-I Hope

Have the audacity to be unfuckwithable.

At some point, the unfuckwithable among us
underwent a "stretching": a "waking up" of sorts.
We broke free of the chains this world placed around us,
and gained a sudden kind of freedom that feels like
bread rising when faced with heat.

We do not stay down.
We do not lay flat.
We rise, rise, rise until there is so much of us
that we overflow, spilling and pouring over
the containers meant to hold us.

We undergo a trial by fire,
and emerge the victor. We echo.
We seek others who are also glitches in the matrix;
we mark them as our tribe.
We have this beautiful way of recognizing
our own awakened kin,
forever united in unfuckwithable "otherness".

-Glitch the Matrix

I am a   p h o e n i x
living in a culture of vultures.

Let them   c i r c l e   overhead.

They cannot   f e a s t upon
what was created to
              e
          s
      i
r
from the *dead.*

                    -Phoenix

The day I made peace with my pain
was the day I was born again.

Pain always speaks,
if you'd only begin listening.

Even your "broken" needs to breathe;
you're allowed to scream
that it hurts when it does.

Press the bruise, kiss the wounds,
they're real.
Feel them, **really** feel them.

For healing,
sit those wounds beside you,
hand them your love,
and show them the sun.

                    -Wounds

There is truth in the form of a s e e d
buried deep beneath your ribcage.

The challenge is to open yourself enough
so as to let it flourish.

You plant it safely inside your heart,
and keep it safe from wildfires
as you slowly bloom into your own "becoming".

You water it with honesty,
understanding, freedom,
space, grace, and patience.
You flood yourself with the nourishment you need to grow.

This is what it means to bloom green,
to truly *claim yourself.*

-Claim

Let yourself go a little wild,
a bit rough around the edges.
The human spirit wasn't meant
for *carefully-curated* perfection.

Desire is a lawless land.
You light yourself on f i r e
hoping you can withstand it.

It   s l o w s   to embers,
and   s c a t e r s   into the wind.

Need is a serrated thing,
the *double-edged sword*
that you either   t h r u s t   or
f
   a
     l
        l
upon.

It consumes until it's g o n e,
but it never goes with grace.

You can be either wholly satiated
or brutally annihilated
by what you burn for.

But in the end,
is the choice ever really *yours*?

                    —Lawless Land

Tonight,
The skies are clearing.
The f i r e   dances flames into my eyes,
the earth hums beneath my feet,
the wind sings hymns to the trees,
the moon stands guard; listening.

I am ready, *molting.*

The second-skin prison
that I've been living in
has loosened just enough
for me to begin   p e e l i n g   it off.

And tonight
I want to throw it on the flames,
and breathe *my own name*
into the   r e s t   of my life.

-The Art of Rising

I know a tired heart,
gritted teeth,
and weary bones
like a   r e l u c t a n t   second-home.

I also know
that when wandering
a
   l
     o
       n
         e   in the dark,
sometimes the way out
begins with just a   s p a r k.

-Spark the Night

I was taught to f e a r my body
as this *shameful* thing.

I was told it was m e n a c i n g,
to ignore its needs.
I was taught to swallow m o d e s t y,
to smile politely, act d e m u r e l y...

and I did (for appearances).

But make NO mistake;
behind the s a f e t y of locked doors,
I explored myself like new terrain.

And when my body b u r n e d hungrily,
I let myself
b
   u
     r
        n   with it

until only ashes were left,
and I was *b r e a t h l e s s.*

−Breathless

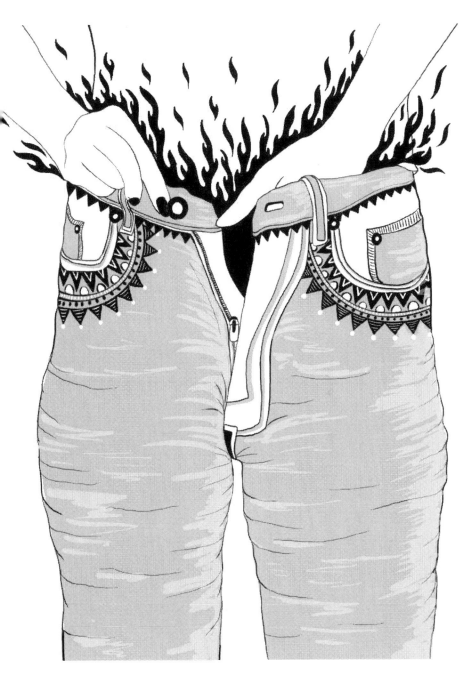

Trauma has deep roots indeed,
but that doesn't mean
you shouldn't pull the weeds.

Anyone or anything
that jeopardizes your healing
must be plucked out immediately.

(The last thing you need are your traumas blooming).

Let your journey and your story
be that of healing and redemption.
Let yours be a tale of growth.
Let your shadow work show for something
by choking out any opportunity for someone or something
to come in and disturb your peace.

Learn your lessons,
count your blessings.
At the FIRST sign of toxicity,
know that it's time to go.
Be decisive in your decisions to avoid backsliding
into dangerous patterns.
Get out before the entire house burns!

Protect yourself.
Tend yourself well.
You owe that to yourself.

-Choose Healing

I go into the forest
to return to myself.

For it is only there
that I can cut through the noise of life
and find the light
that still glows deep inside of me.

I sometimes need reminding
that everything is   c-o-n-n-e-c-t-e-d.

Every one of us matters.
Each one of us is sacred.

-Sacred Souls

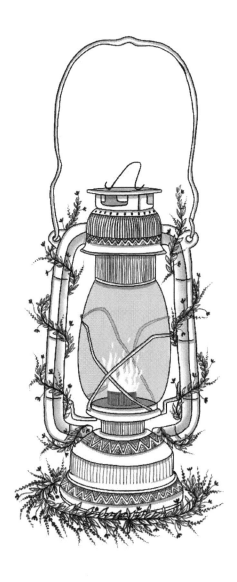

You have so much fire left inside of you
to give to this world.

Don't you dare give up now.

Where are my soft souls,
never held captive by their ego,
who love without end,
who have known pain
but refuse to inflict it?

We burn like embers
in a gentle wind:
empathetic and compassionate.

-Forged by Fire

It was a l o n g time coming,
but I took every hole in the surface of my skin,
opened by pain, loss, grief, and anxiety,
and I seeded each of them, so *delicately*.

After a long winter (and lack of fire),
in the spring; w i l d f l o w e r s.

-Wildflowers

When I committed to the   f l a m e s
what was *never mine* in the first place,
all that was left standing was me.

I am   b e t t e r   than ever,
without the weight of things
that were never mine to
c   y.
   a   r
      r

        -Better Than Ever

One day, I hope you find someone
who starts a fire within you that never dies.

I hope that someone
is YOU.

May sunbeams ignite your dreams,
may you love like a firestorm,
and may light and warmth
never turn their back on you.

                    —Love & Light

Every day,
I   d-i-v-i-d-e   up the pieces of myself,
feeling about as useful as a spent match.
I wouldn't know where they belong,
so it would be rude to even ask.

Guided by confusion (or delusion),
I dice myself into
p
  i
e
  c
e
  s,
and ration them into others' hands.

I always end up cutting off my own,
then wonder why I am left holding *nothing*.

I don't know how to keep me.
How do you teach that?
How do you learn to choose what nobody ever has?

                   -"Damaged" Goods

An open letter to myself:

I am sorry I put you through hell,
sorry I didn't love you enough,
sorry I put you on the back burner so long,
and sorry I never forgave what you couldn't change.

You did the best you could with what you had,
and I am proud of you for that.

I promise that I am here now,
and though we have grown a lot since then,
I promise that I will love the parts of me
that you still inhabit.

             -Forgiveness

You said you would like to see the whole world burn,
down,

d
o
w
n

to a mere pile of ashes you could land in.

Some days, you fear there is nothing good left;
that humans destroy everything,
and hope is too *exhausting*.

I know it feels like you are   s u f f o c a t i n g.

But, my friend, I would sit in the ashes with you any day,
and I would hold you whole again.

-Whole

You were born with a voice inside your head
that was created to keep you steady.

If ever that voice whispers
that what you have is not what you deserve,
listen like your life depends on it.

This voice is your most loyal friend,
the flame that burns without end,
the extension of your consciousness.

Listen.

Never ask a woman with *fire* in her belly
to settle for a steady diet of breadcrumbs.

Her   h u n g e r   will become her,
and she will be a sight to behold
the moment she *learns her worth*.

One day, you will regret not feeding her spirit,
but by then...
she will have *long forgotten* your name.

-Breadcrumbs

May all your toxic patterns be broken,

and always by your own hand.

Standing in your power
will terrify many people.
You become a human flame:
formidable, intimidating,
and inspiring all at once.

You become a mirror
for the journey of others:
the force of nature
that they too *could* become.

                    -Power

I remember when I was younger,
the other kids would play a game
called "Fuck, Marry, Kill".

I'd listen to the names of my other classmates
rattled off like grocery lists:
as if they understood what any of it meant.

They were correct about something:
when they said my name, they said "Kill".
Don't fuck her.
Don't marry her.
She's not the type for either!
She's a strange kind of "other",
and definitely a little dangerous.
Kill her bold.
Kill her power.
Kill her mouth.
Kill her fire.
Kill her,
or she might kill you.

You don't take me home for a night:
you absorb me into your bones for a lifetime,
and I don't wash out of your mouth soap;
you'll taste me wherever you go.
Don't marry me:
I'll call your mother on her bullshit,
skip Sunday dinner for a solo walk in the forest,
and end up naming all the trees.

I'm older now.
I've fucked, I've married,
but I haven't been killed yet.

Nobody has ever had the balls to do it.

-Fuck, Marry, Kill

I am not a simple convenience.
I am wildly, utterly disruptive.
If you're searching for still waters,
steer clear of my rough seas.

I am so tired of pretending
you can be less than a living storm
and still
        stand
                beside
                        me.

                -In Over Your Head

Never is my spirit better at belonging
than with a forest floor
beneath my bare feet,
velvet moss coaxing the "weary"
from my deeply-aching bones.

I sit by the fire,
and allow the trees to sing me back home
to the lullabies inside my   s o u l.

-Forest Floor

My head lives up in the   c l o u d s;
my feet remain upon the   g r o u n d.

Magick surrounds and moves me,
but I'm rooted firmly in reality.

I am the steady, stoic voice of   r e a s o n
who ebbs and flows like tides and seasons.

I am the embodiment of an *eternal*   f l a m e
who still craves the cool of crashing waves.

-Oxymoron

Inside of me lives a compass,
and I am never directionless.

The needle is on fire,
guiding me to the *home* within myself
that blazes due North
until the stars   b u r n   out.

—Compass

I plant my feet in the damp earth,
rain-soaked and full of twilight.
The winds swirl my hair into my eyes,
though I am blind to nothing here.

I sway with the flames to evensong.
I chant away the day,
and welcome the night with open arms.

-Forest Witch

The next time you think yourself a god,
remember this:
I am godless, a *goddess*.

My heaven is a place that ties your tongue,
and I fall
to
    my
        k n e e s   for no one,
but I will have you on yours so frequently
that they will bleed for me.

You see,
I am everything.

I am a u n i v e r s e on my own,
and I have learned never to make a home
in any place that cannot hold the light
that is my *birthright*.

-Goddess

Today,
I seek what seeks me.
I hold what holds me.
I love what loves me.

Today,
I release what does not serve me.
I call forth the strength I need for healing.
I begin a new journey.

May clarity light my way,
today and always.

I've tried to bring my shadows into the light,
but they tell me they were born for hiding.

Still, I go looking for them,
and hope beyond all hoping
that I one day find them
lying dead among some ruins,
caved in under the weight of love.

For now,
I turn my face to the sun
and pray it is **enough**.

-Sunflower

Stars above,
how old am I?
This cannot be my first or only lifetime.

I am silver droplets of   u n i v e r s e.
I am made of equal parts fire and earth.

I am a galaxy of longing,
yearning for what has been
swimming in my   s o u l
for so much longer than I could *ever remember*.

-Old Soul

Young heart,
old soul:
the best of both worlds.

I am childlike innocence
and timeless wisdom.

This allows me to see the truth in everything;
this is what keeps my fire burning.

                    -Dichotomy

As I have aged,
I have learned the fine art of the slow-burn.

I now understand that what is worth my time
need not reduce me to cinders.

I can contain my passion in a safe, calculated way
that allows me to save some energy for myself.

When I fall,
I
f
   a
     l
       l   so hard
that the ground gives way
beneath the weight
of my every insecurity;
I do nothing *halfway*.

So, whenever I do *break*,

I   s-h-a-t-t-e-r   with the force
of warring worlds ending,
my pain an *apocalyptic* event
stretching to the edges
of an oblivion spinning
like the needle of a compass.

-The Fallen

It's been so long now
that I've been sitting still,
watching the world turning around me.
Am I hopeless?
Am I listless?
Am I a   l o s t   cause?

I know what is at stake,
but I cannot   m o v e   at all.

One foot in front of the other:
it just seems so impossible,
until I remember just how many times
I have gotten up off the ground before.

So please,
give me just a moment
to remind myself
that I am still meant for   *m o r e*   *than this.*

                    -More

```
I spent years languishing
In a slow -
          B
          U
          R
          N
          I
          N
          G        house
hidden deep within my mind,
forever unable to leave
my grief and    t r a u m a    behind.

I    c-o-l-l-a-g-e-d    my pain
onto walls in the hall,
and I stared years into it all;
unable to move.

I later learned...
there were *greener pastures*
waiting to be found:
all I ever had to do
was turn around.
```

                    -Greener Pastures

Winter saw me lose my way;
frozen thorn and rose   *d e c a y e d.*
Dead stems became
                                    g
                            n
                        i
                    b
                m
            i
        l
    c
vines; to bind my feet to where I remained standing.

I tried to leave my body, but it felt too h e a v y.

Ice weighs so much more than freedom.
I did not move for months.

I cursed *grey* sky and prayed for f i r e *red,*
frozen to the *white* of bone.
I dreamed of spring, *greener* things,
the boldness of autumn *gold,*
and the *orange* of an Indian summer.

I had forgotten the sun.
Luckily, it had not forgotten me.

                    -The Longest Winter

The sun does not apologize for her light;
even if it burns your eyes, it will shine.

The sky does not does not fear being deep and wide
or falling when it's time to cry.

The leaves show us that it's okay to wither away
as the time comes for season's change.

The moon proves that it's still just as powerful
during each of its numerous phases.

The tides show that you can push and pull,
and still remain a constant...

So why should YOU be any different?

Be relentless in defense of
keeping your own energy pure.
Do not allow anyone in
who will only pollute it.
If you don't want to live a mediocre life,
you have to refuse *mediocre bullshit.*

-Safeguard

If we are what we love,
then I am motes of s t a r d u s t.
I am the gravity of creative velocity,
and the axis that *turns* my curiosity.

I am the luminosity of a crescent moon,
and the impossible **fire** of the sun.
I am the color palette of every   s u n s e t,
the itching wanderlust of *unrest.*

I am sweet French vanilla coffee,
and the *morning scent* of parchment.
I am mid-August by the ocean,
and an   h o u r g l a s s   turned over.

I am   r e b e l l i o n, cognac leather,
long earrings made of feathers.
I am foaming bubbles in a bath,
glass of wine; *poetry book* in my hand.

I am sweet tea on a June front porch,
the reliable   f l a m e   that keeps you warm.

-Identity

When I finally *burn out*
and my story has reached its   e n d,
scatter my ashes in the ocean,
sing my name *into the wind.*

I'll come back to you then,
and curl up inside your heart
until Time calls you home.
Keep me safe, and I will wait for you.

                    -Scatter

I could be standing in a field,
lush and green and *lovely,*
but my head always tricks me
into thinking
all
        is
             b u r n i n g.

                        -Trickster

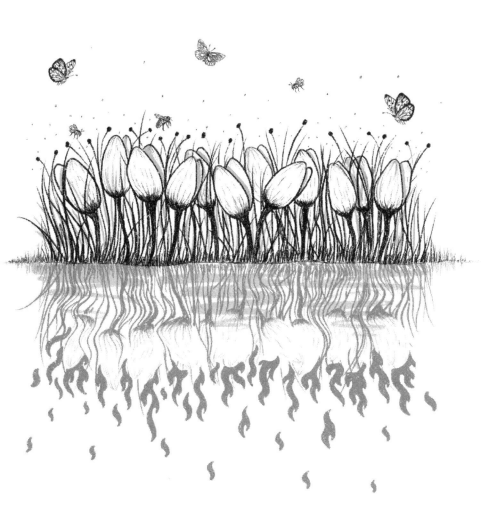

How I can have
the raging desire inside of me
to help others at the expense
of my own well-being
is both awe-inspiring
and *terrifying*.

-Back Burner

It is not your responsibility
to burn yourself out
to keep someone else around.

You might be a phoenix,
but you can reduce the number of times
that you are called to rise from ashes.

                -Controlled Burning

Strength and strong will
are not only shown by
h
    a
       n
          g
       i
    n
g
on until the end
by bloody fingertips.

Sometimes,
strength looks down at the stones below,
quietly closes its eyes,
and jumps into letting go.

-Free Fall

Far too often,
I cut myself *open*
with the fiery blows
of my own
     c r u e l
          w o r d s.

From now on,
I will treat myself as I deserve.

    -Self-Inflicted Wounds

I know that I am strong,
that I have weathered many storms,
but some days, it's hard to rise.

Some days,
I have a hard time summoning my fire and fight,
and I spend too much time drowning inside my mind.

It is always then that I wonder if it is possible
to sink any lower than the floor.
Thoughts creep in like vapored poison.

I try to remember that I never stay down for long.
In those moments, that is enough.

Heaven and Hell can look curiously like porcelain,
when your body suddenly revolts,
and your existence feels like a burdenous waste.

You sit with   b u r n i n g, cold-sweat chills,
and toss back your stuck-throat pills,
hoping to return to *something resembling normalcy.*

At least when you are physically ill,
you know it needs to *run its course,*
before you are restored to whatever came before.

But when it's your own traitorous brain telling you
that you are *on fire,* and only the floor is safe?
You tend to   s t a y.

You build homes in tile grout-lines.
You call your "feel fine" body a   l i a r,
and allow your bones to fuse with rug fibers.

You think "Just let me die here",
but you cannot sink *any lower than the floor.*

Meanwhile, the world *awaits your return*
on the   *o t h e r   s i d e*   of the door.

                    -The Other Side of the Door

We go through life demanding apologies
for micro-wrongdoings
that sometimes don't even exist outside of our own egos.
Is ignorance truly bliss?

We give no one a chance; not even ourselves,
but we expect others to love us perfectly and well.
We get hypersensitive, illogical, irrational:
falling into a wound we dug into our own misdirection,
and then retreat into a shell we built-
shiny, but paper-thin, and underprotective.

We break our own ribcages when someone breaks our heart,
because we have never perfected the art
of   s t r e t c h i n g   them.
We close off when we should open,
fall silent when we should have spoken,
and hope beyond all hoping
that we look like we know what we are doing,
even though we KNOW nobody ever does.

What DO we want?

Sometimes I wonder if any of us know
how to do anything but self-sabotage:
we trash ourselves, our friendships,
our partners, our jobs, our surroundings,
and wonder why we're DROWNING, and chronically unhappy.

So, stop throwing yourself into the fire,
and manifest your desires into truth.

It's time to grab healing by the "hope",
and tell your chest that it is warm,
and tell your heart that it is home,
and tell YOURSELF that you are whole.

Because, fellow human,
what you DECIDE you are,
is all you'll ever truly own upon this earth.
So transcend your ego,
and learn to feed your soul.

-Evolve

93

This is your reminder
to set your   o w n   narrative,
and never, NEVER
let anyone *take a lighter*
to the edges of your pages.

                    -Set Your Narrative

I was never one for niceties;
for slurped coffee and cheap conversation.
I care nothing for the weather, and I know the time.
I am one for the deep, the *sublime,*
the exchanges that can change hearts and   m i n d s.

Stay here a while,
sit   b e s i d e   me.

Tell me of your *dreams* and what lights you on **fire.**
Let us connect with more than a
p-a-s-s-i-n-g
g
l
a
n
c
e.

Hear me, and let me speak hope into your desires.
Let's see one another, let's *really* look,
and see clearly the beauty that only ever comes
from the   g e n u i n e.

Let us enter as strangers,
leave as *friends.*

                    -Connectivity

I wear vulnerability like a *velvet cloak.*

I am rich in my ability to be o p e n,
a glorious mix of strong and delicate.

I am candlelight,
trailing dress,
and **madness.**

I am tears and p a s s i o n never lost,
the strength it takes to remain *soft.*

-Vulnerability

Some days,
I wonder if I'm doing it all wrong,
when all I ever want to do
is get it right...

Is it enough to try?

Can a phoenix raise a dove?

I am a wildfire raising a meadow,
trying to give her room to bloom.

I hear the murmur of my now-gone father:
"One day, you're going to have a daughter,
and she's going to be just like you!"
In weak moments, I wish that were true...

Maybe then I would know the right things to do.

For now, I can only hope and dream
that someday, she will crave my flames,
and I will need her peace.

In the meantime, I will trail the wake
of her gentle, springtime rain,
trying not to get in her way.

I, her mother, the scorched-earth summer,
will keep walking
(probably a bit too close) behind her...

armed with love and fire.

-The Phoenix and the Dove

Above: an orange **fire** sky.
Below: a g h o s t l y   boat upon the bay,
late in the breezy waning of July,
I stare at the horizon and curse the skies.

This night looks like my father's l a s t.
The sky then looked just like this,
and he never saw his *untimely* end coming,
(though I suppose nobody ever did).

He saw only a perfect night, a f l a w l e s s sunset,
and I'm sure he believed he had *many left*.

All I know,
is I would *swallow the sun* whole
to bring him home again.

-Late July

Death and grief are so strange;
they re-arrange you on a molecular level.
They stay with you, and I have found that I am unable
to let them go, even for a moment.

"It gets easier".
(That's what they promised me).
They were wrong, but as for what it gets
(if not "easier"),
I have no words to define that.

The most it does is fade around the edges.
The burning becomes a gnawing, an ache
that remains for the rest of your days.

I am tired, and much changed.

But, this ache?
If it reminds me of *you*...let it stay.

If the past is a *pile of ashes*,
how do I turn it into something l a s t i n g?

My mind lost within it,
I fashion these memories into beads,
and place each of them
upon a   s-t-r-i-n-g.

My mother still *dreams.*
My father still **breathes.**
My siblings run after me,
chasing daylight.
A boy kisses me,
and I close my eyes *just in time.*
There are feet pounding parallel to pines,
riverbeds and campfires,
swift dives and cold swims.
There are   t r e a s u r e d   grandparents,
stage-whispered secrets,
and the comfort of purrs and whiskers.
There are summer homes,
and balconies, and boxed moments
encased in the *burnt amber* of sunsets.
There is a long white gown,
and a bouquet of flowers.
There's the sound of new, shrill cries.

There are lullabies,
and pain,
and heartbreak,
and wisdom,
and love,
and loss,
and hope.

When finished,
I k-n-o-t   t-h-e   s-t-r-i-n-g
as though it's the end of my   r-o-p-e...

But when placed around my neck,
I do not hang by it.
It's no g a l l o w s.

It is *all I am*,
and all I've known:
an h e i r l o o m.

-Heirloom

Combust

(the heart)

I must learn when and how to put my love
D
   O
     W
       N.
But how?
How could I ever put you away
when each heartbeat screams out *your name*,
when every desperate breath that burns my lungs
infuses my blood with you again?

You are the very life of me,
and you will surely be the   d e a t h   of me.

My own veins swim with you unendingly,
So tell me, then,
when do I stop bleeding for you?

-Bleeding Out

I would throw down

r
 o
o
 t
s

with you
if I ever had the   c h a n c e.

We'd grow   s t r o n g   in tender shoots,
and bloom in
                   burning
                             lands.

-Roots

We were the g n a w   of an unfinished song,
a dusty book with a
f
   o
     l
      d
    e
d
page.

We were a verbal eclipse, an   e l l i p s e s...
waiting to be continued again.

We were the story, the lyrics,
the fire   b-e-t-w-e-e-n   lines
that we once longed to *live* inside.

But we ended our sentences with question marks,
and we can't *remember* the reasons   w h y.

               -We

Can hope b l o o m   in flames or shade?
Can Time give back what it *takes away*?
I once saw the *answers to life* in your eyes,
now I can only remember how to say   g o o d b y e.

                        -Amnesia

I'll take the *birthmarks*
of this life I've lived,
connect them into
c o n s t e l l a t i o n s.

When I do,
I'll search for you.

Whatever the Universe is,
you and I are made of it:
shared dust from *blazing*
                s t a r s.

When reborn,
we will **reunite**
under
        the

            n   o
      a   p
c   y
of starlight.

When we do,
bless this *cosmic skin*,
by stargazing upon it
with your   f i n g e r t i p s.

Tell me we will never *end*.

                    —Cosmic Skin

You and me:
a shared fate and sacred destiny,
joined for all of Time.

I will never cast you aside.
I will never leave your side.

Where you go,
I go.

Your   d a r k n e s s
does not scare me,
nor will I run from you.

Like a shooting star,
I'm falling for

the   p h a s e s   of your moon ☾ .

                    -Nocturnal

I have spent enough time with darkness
to know it intimately.
It has never frightened me.

I carry so much of it within,
but I wear hope like stars that shine
through the black.

Because of that,
there is nothing you could say or do
that would send me running.
Share with me your dark, your shadows.
I will love you all the more for them.

I can build you a fire,
and I have plenty of starlight to spare.

I want to draw   h e a r t s   on your palms
with my unsteady fingers.

I want to count your lashes
as you quietly *dream.*

Then, I want to wake you,
and let you *have your*
w   a   y
with me...

until the glow of the moon
gives way to the flaming *vestiges*
of sun and   m o r n i n g.

                    -Want

"I would *take your hand*,
and walk with you
through f i r e."

No,
that's *inadequate*; a tired cliché.
You are worth so much more
than more of the same.

Let me try that again:

"I would you hold you high *above the* f l a m e s,
and become the human

    t
  o r
    c
    h

that *l i g h t s*   your way."

                    —Human Torch

The first time I felt your h e a t,
I began melting right into *you*.

Ever since our *unexpected* osmosis,
I cannot   e x t r a c t
my molecules from yours.

We   r a i n e d   down upon one another years before,
and after all this time,
we're still   p u d d l e s   on the floor.

                  -Worth Melting For

You may have let go of my hand; of our love,
but you could never let go of your hold on my heart.

There will always be room left for you.

Maybe all we were meant to be
is beautifully *unfinished.*

Maybe we are a story
without a true ending:
a love
h
   a
      n
        g
          i
          n
          g
in the balance,
still   i n c a n d e s c e n t,
never fully extinguished.

-Unfinished

You took my rigid heart
in its fortress of a ribcage,
and taught it to   s t r e t   c   h;
to break just the *right way.*

You taught me to soften,
to open,
to

            e
      s
   i
r
and
f
a
l
l
like the sun.

You left me open,
yet *perfectly undone.*

                    –Perfectly Undone

Show me that love need not come with brutality.
Show me that we can enjoy the   j o u r n e y
without fixating on an ending.
Show me how to *light up like a candle*
in the shadows of the late hours.

Show me how to dream like the sky,
deep and wide and open
like a flower not knowing it's in bloom.
Show me that love can look like me and you...

in this moment;
as
      we
          a r e.

                    —Show Me

This is a finite world,
full of boundaries and complacency.
But *you light everything on fire,*
and I would
b
   u
     r
        n
to worship the infinite in you.

I would gladly herald your arrival
as the *trail of ashes* in your wake,
if it meant you would hold me in your hands,
and sing my bones to   d e a t h.

I would whisper your name
into the
f   s
  o   d
    l
of the wind
as I scattered away.

You are *annihilating.*

—Trail of Ashes

You fell into my forbidden forest eyes,
and I hung my life on the corner of your smile.

We set this whole world on fire
with nothing but the friction of our skin.

I miss so many things, but most of all...

I miss the way we never needed to say anything.

I miss the way you always *knew.*

The roots of my best dreams
are still watered by the   m e m o r y   of you,
and I've tried to outrun the *truth*
until my heels b u r n and
b
   l
      e
        e
          d,
but I cannot move from the spot
where *you planted me.*

My   w-i-n-g-s-p-a-n   is exactly your arms' length,
and I just do not have the strength
to leave the place I last was in them.

-Wingspan

There is a unique kind of pain that exists
right before it truly ends.

It hits you that you laid waste
to your love some time ago,
and have just been complacently waiting
for the fire to catch.

So, when it *finally* burns,
why does it <u>still</u> manage to hurt?

You couldn't bring yourself to be what I need,
but I never truly considered
that you might also be h u r t i n g.

I now fear that my *empathy*
was only ever extended to me.

I am sorry if I was so busy *burning my pain at the stake*
that I forgot how to be h u m a n to you,

because there was a time when you were good to me, too.

I think you are a good person,
if a little broken in ways I cannot fix.

I set
d
   o
     w
       n
my own disappointment.
I *barely resist* the urge to pick it back up.

Instead, I pick up f o r g i v e n e s s.
It weighs a lot less.

                    —Forgiveness

In you, I experienced true *surrender.*

Every wall I'd ever rendered
managed to destroy itself,
either burned up or
drowned
                 down
                                deep
in the wells of tears I used to weep
for the loss
                 of
                      lesser
                              l o v e s.

                    -White Flag

The *crumpled* d r e s s
in the back of my closet
that I last made love to you in
smells of you,
and my perfume, and *nostalgic regret.*

I long to water it with my tears;
see if we somehow grow back.

Instead, I rip it to shreds,
and b u r n it.

-The Dress

Oh, what a directionless calamity:
you came in *without a w a r n i n g*
to love me tragically, and then just leave.
And now I am wounded too deeply
to see the forest for the trees.

I hear   c h a i n s a w s   in my dreams.
If a tree
f
   a
     l
       l
         s
unexpectedly in a forest,
felled by the breeze of *bated breathing*,
with no one around to hear but me,
was it real or make believe?

Were WE...?

I sleep in beds of *burning leaves*,
hoping that regret left on a doorstep last September 15th
would have you falling again
                              toward
                                        me,
but you don't, and I know you won't.

I am shivering, and you look everywhere
except at me.

If you ever need me;
if it's ever me you're missing,
I'm under the doormat where you last left me,
Growing roots down into concrete,
a sapling starving for   *k i n d e r   g r a v i t y.*

Like the dirt beneath your feet,
you just keep stepping on me.
But it sure is nice to keep watching you leave,
because I always know you're coming home...

I just wish it were to *me.*

-Kinder Gravity

Distance sits between us,
frost collects on stuck-tongue love.
Winter sets in, unforgiving:
heart and hearth u n u s e d and *cold.*

There is no warm expansion,
just numb, reckless abandon.
We do not die with d i g n i t y:
we hold our breath and *call it breathing.*

Finally;
the e x h a l e.

Breathe out...
we heat the air,
but not our s o u l s.

A   g l a c i e r   blooms between us.

Look how *f a r* we've come.

-Winter Cold

"Ashes", we once thought,
but the   e m b e r s   in our eyes
might have *bought us time.*

                    -Embers

Writing of you is a bloodletting;
tears and ink bleeding our story
onto pages where our combustible love still lives.

One day, the broken quill will   p i e r c e
the chambers of my heart *like a dagger*,
and I will
s
 t
a
 g
g
 e
r
into the next life,
still refusing to leave you   b e h i n d.

Follow the devotion in my words like a map,
and *come find me again.*

Maybe then you'll **never let me go.**

                    -Bloodletting

I am trapped and frozen
in the very moment when you left.
I am crushed ice and s h e d skin,
a *molted shell* that melts within;
a spent shell casing.

I am an emptiness, a h o l l o w–
standing at the edge of a cliff:
joints *bone-stiff*; lantern in hand,
staring out at a lighthouse that *doesn't exist*.

The dark seas
　　　　e,
　　　s
　　i
　r
and I am swallowed into n o t h i n g.

-Ghost Lighthouse

The winds of *change* took our vessel,
and ran it   a g r o u n d
on   u n f a m i l i a r   shores.

I had *just enough fight* left
to light a   t o r c h, burn the ship,
and with one, last   g o o d b y e,
walk
a
   w
      a
         y
from it.

From you.
From us.

                    -Shipwreck

I never imagined there'd be you without me,
now all I have are memories,

and they are gradually *fading*...

    -You are Slipping Away

Your silences,
they always   s c r e a m,

yet it's your voice
that still wakes the dead in me.

The absence of you:
it doesn't always scream.

Sometimes, it floats and creeps.

It is the faint chill left unmoored
by the crack in the door you *closed* on us.

It is the wispy vapor of lost love.

It is the unavoidable reopening of our coffin,
the one I often sneak out into the graveyard
to
    lie
        in,
in a barren land of souls and bones,
where only I am haunted.

I drop my lantern on the edge of the granite,
wondering why damp and stone are never warm...
y o u   were.

Your absence, it softly lingers.
It curls around me: a crooked finger,
a ring snagging a favorite sweater.
When I cut the pulled thread,
it never *looks quite right* again.
You are that one piece always m i s s i n g.

I have learned with time,
that your absence has its own h e a r t b e a t,
and it sometimes *replaces mine.*

        -Void

Can I break our soul-tie
the way you broke my heart...

slowly and invisibly,
then   s-e-v-e-r-e-d   all at once?

I burned for you *constantly*
thinking love would be   e n o u g h;

you wined and dined my promises,
though I held an *empty cup.*

You soon
d
r
o
p
p
e
d
my hand,
and took off *running for your life*,

and in the wake of your   c r u e l   haste,
you ran away with mine.

                    -Soul-Tie

My witching hour
is right before midnight;
"Let me just see what he's doing..."

Cracked phone screen,
filtered glow and wasted dreams:
you're smiling, but never at me.
You haven't checked my stories,
but half of them were meant for you.

They'll disappear shortly, like you always do.

You breathe without me
in some space far away.
You listen for the sound
of my heart breaking again
to make sure you still hold me.

Silence is your weaponry.
I burn,
and
I
bleed.

                    —Witching Hour

At the end of the day,
why else are we here
if not to absolutely, completely,
utterly burn for another?
Why do we curse the very existence
of the one face we cannot forget
because remembering it hurts
just as badly as forgetting it?
Why do we cry at the end of films
when the love depicted stirs our blood
in the direction of the one
we will never be able to let go of?
Why do we find that one person
inside every song we hear,
and end up on the side of the road,
heaving rivers over the steering wheel?
Why do we wake from fever dreams
paralyzed and gasping to breathe
around the sinkhole in our chests
where their head once rested?
Why do we hold a single name so sacred
that our mind screams it
when our lips say someone else's?
Why do we feel their presence
like a phantom, twisted limb,
somehow with us yet simultaneously gone
and aching, aching,
aching down to the bone?
How can it be that we go on living
while burning alive,
knowing all the while
that Time is both healer and thief,
that there is no separating
what was always, always *meant to be?*

-To Burn for Another

I will *always* burn for you.

There is nowhere you could go
that I wouldn't want to follow.
There is no lifetime you could live
where I wouldn't look for you again.

This is beyond us...
our collision a cosmic event;
predestined.

-Predestined

It's you and I for all of time.

Our shared soul binds us
by glow of moon and light of stardust.
We are fused anew, reunited,
blessed whole by the Universe.

-Divine

I think of you...
and the pain,
the past,
and the chain of events
that led us back together
all settle into perfect alignment.

We are something
carved of the divine.

In the elusive throes of sleep,
my eyelids flutter
like butterfly's wings.

Behind them, we   d a n c e   again.

When the music stops,
you   k i s s   me.

I wake, lips stinging.

                    -Dreamland

You're the eye of every storm,
the lifeboat on my lips.

I float upon your rolling sea,
though I do not fear the drowning.

I fix my eyes to the sapphire sky...

even the stars fall for you,
and I am not the least bit surprised.

                    -You

I will find you again, my f l a m e.
I will chase you through time.
I will search   r e l e n t l e s s l y
until I find *my own fire*
reflected back through *your eyes.*

      -Relentless

You,
my fire,
my embers, my flame,
the one that my midnight lips
find like footfalls in the earth.

You,
my rebirth,
my spring, my awakening,
r
      a
           i
                n
your gilded honey over me
in slow, sweet-nothinged breath.

Let me catch my death
in your transcendent arms.

-Awakening

We are ancient, you and I.

It's like the skies orchestrated our return
to the one place we can always call "home":
our ancient, timeless love.

What the Universe joins together
can never be undone.

It seems like yesterday
you came   c a r e e n i n g   into my
 o   t
r   i
   b
with your usual lack of grace.

Now, years later
here I stay...

still trying to fetch my face from your flames.

                    -Fetch My Face

The fine line that lies
between love and lust
is as thin as the divide
that never existed between us.

-Fiendfyre

I crave the   s w e e t e s t   annihilation,
to undo and
u
 n
r
 a
v
 e
l
you,

to raise an army against you in bed,
you   b r e a t h l e s s   against the thunder in my chest
that you claim as your throne.

I call "home" the silence between your heartbeats.

Give me magnificent chaos, the   c o n q u e r i n g:
mind, body, and soul tied to me for *eternity*.
Let us *set fire to one another* and destroy the earth,

forever   r u i n e d   for anyone else.

-Ruin

You b u r n e d   the promise of forever
into my brain,
and now my lips will only
speak
         your
                 name.

                    -Lip Service

I want to kiss life into your skin,
worshipping it with all my strength.

So speak to me in breathless sighs,
and make my
  g
    a
      s
        p
          s
your lullabies.

-Resplendent

I take you with me everywhere I go.
You live   d e e p   within my very skin,
above the din of quiet that whispers
its faucet-drip existence.

Your face shines behind my eyes,
your hands reach for my dreams;
pulling me back into your memory
until I slip into you; losing my footing.

Calling me back to you is as *easy as breathing...*
you whisper my name and I come running.
I will   a l w a y s   rush back to your side;
to light the embers you hold within my mind.

No one else will ever stand a chance.

-Never Far

When it's her
                s
            k
        a
    e
p

and

v
    a
      l
        l
          e
            y
              s
you're exploring,
when it's her eyes *you lose yourself* inside...

do you ever let your resolve slip,
and imagine that they're   m i n e ?

                -Flashback

Oh, for those moments
where humans become flames...

We look into the eyes of another,
and run our fingers along their skin.

The hunger lights the wick:
we combust and consume.

Tonight,
I will k i l l all the lights.

Moon and fire in my eyes,
I will deliberately
take
          my
                 t i m e.

I'll voraciously learn you
like a second language,

I'll hungrily m-a-p out your skin
with the *tip of my tongue.*

By the time morning c o m e s,
I will speak you fluently.

                 -Second Language

And in that moment
when we transferred our energies,
fire upon fire, skin meeting skin,
eyes seeing the synchronicity of everything,
there was a breaking.

We died unto our separate selves,
and dove straight into the night,
reunited recognition eclipsing lifetimes,
bound by the gold of starlight.

                    -Recognition

If you ask me what it's like
to hold the world within my palms,
I will always say it feels like _you_.

No matter how dark it gets,
no matter how uncertain life is,
in your arms, everything g l o w s.

You are my living sunrise.

We h-o-l-d one another without touch.

We are intimate
                despite
                        d i s t a n c e,
and we breathe
as one
with separate lungs.

In the still of the night,
I   c l o s e   my eyes
and there you are, *beside me.*

Time and space are nothing at all.

                    -Transcendent

You ruined everything, you know.
After you, my carefully calibrated world
crashed and burned around me.

Cynicism, skepticism,
my tendency to believe in nothing:
after you, they all disappeared.

All there was, was magic.
You made the impossible undeniable,
and I will never recover.

There is always a place for you in my story.
I will   a l w a y s   find a way to write you in:
footnotes, edges, margins,
they cannot contain you
or hold how much you mean.

I love you **in bold;**
in whole   n o v e l s.

You could burn the book,
but the ashes would find a way
to re-write our love.

                    -Title Case

You were heaven for my senses,
our separation: hell.
The agony should not surprise me,
given how hard I fell.

Leaving was the kindest thing
either of us could have done.
If we want to find ourselves again,
we must not keep in touch.

-Separation

It's not that I no longer love you,
part of me will always burn for you.

But it would be the ruin of me to forget
the way you broke me when you left.

I have to learn to live without you,
so please *never come back.*

A friend of mine recently had a dream,
where she found me in whimsical surroundings,
standing sadly amidst a floral sea:
the wilted, staring at the blooming.

I couldn't bring myself to touch them,
afraid it might change the ending.

She asked me who they were from,
and I quietly told her your name.
"Wasn't that what you wanted?"
My eyes spoke for me: "Too little, too late".

Gently, she told me
that she thinks this means
you still love me front and center,
but I can't remember what that felt like.

They were exactly what I would have loved
if you had delivered them yourself,
if you had stayed.

But you didn't. So I set fire to them instead.

-Secondhand Dream

Our story
b l e e d s
from my burning eyes
until I cannot tell
stars from s t r e e t l i g h t s.

-Blur

The playlist we made
plays softly in my dreams,
and there we are again:
falling,
falling,
f a l l i n g.

By now,
the unending ache of your absence
has silently eclipsed
our small piece of forever.

The pain is now familiar
and aches so deeply,
that I can't recall
what came before the burning.

How will I ever learn to breathe
around the you-shaped-space beside me?

-You-Shaped-Space

I find you most easily *in the shadows:*
candles in the rain,
we sway.

We dance
t
  o
    w
    a
  r
d
one another again,
poised at the ready
to
    n e v e r
         let
            go
even though we know
that we play a losing game.

-Sore Losers

Win or lose or crash-and-burn;
I still choose you.

I will love you boundlessly,
without condition,
without regard to time or distance.

The b i t t e r truth is you're the roots of me,
and I don't want this overgrown garden,
untended and wild, to need weeding.

Foolishly picking our charred, weedy remains,
I'm ready to place them in a dusty vase
and call them flowers.

They won't bloom like I wish they would;
a weed cannot become a rose.

I should have left them   a l o n e.

-By Any Other Name

I can't erase the truth,
and it's all I long to do.

You leave traces of you everywhere,
and in the air, I feel you breathe
elsewhere on this earth,
yet
      somehow   beside
                   me.

I think of how you softly you ruined me,
and how unnerving an undoing can be
when you never see it coming.

          -An Undoing

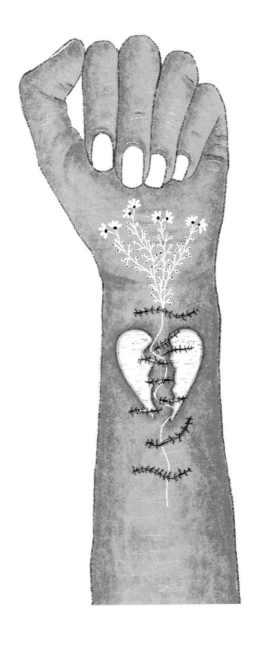

Heart-shaped wounds
are the only ones that never fully close.

Instead, they   b l o o m,
and the grief we're given
continues to burn through
any new scar tissue
stubborn enough to
                w.
        o
     r
g

There are small c-r-a-c-k-s
that will always show.

                    -Heart-Shaped-Wounds

Moth to flame,
I fly straight into the sun
to
h
u
r
l
myself in your general direction.

You glow,
I follow.

                    -Luna Moth

I burn the midnight oil thinking of you.
There's something about the dark that makes
falling into you so damn effortless.

You are the root of all my sleepless nights,
and the dark cannot hide my every thought of you.

You might as well be the moon.

You are the lifeline
that I never knew I always had.

We are infinitely   c-o-n-n-e-c-t-e-d.

We are one,
and I'd give up half the lives I've yet to live

just to find you in the next.

-Invisible String

You held my face in your hands, wondering;
"Where have you been all my life?"

I thought about it for a moment,
pondering the design of divine timing
that pulled our cable cars
along a chain we couldn't see,
orchestrating this; our intersecting.

I smiled, and I replied
"Waiting for my Destiny to find me."

You kissed me with stars in your eyes,
and I held onto you like you
        g
     n
  u
h
the moon.

              -Destiny

Your love sits beside me
in the rough, the dark, the ugly.
You catch erratic tears
and scrape my body off of floors
when grief collapses it.
You steady ragged breaths
and stop death from my heart,
loving me despite my scars.
You are here when it matters,
and real love kneels in the real:
it does not know of doors,
only of windows, of sky,
of skin and soul and breath and life.
When I am strong and you in need,
I'll mosaic your broken pieces
as you have always done for me.
This love magics the mundane;
knows the whole truth, and stays.

-This Love

May we always look out of windows together,
and see no storm we cannot weather.

May we seek *nothing but scenery* in looking out,
and find stillness from the loud.

May we daydream not of greener pastures,
but of the glow of continued laughter.

May we always know
that "unconditional" is a place called "home".

May we remember that real love
is something not felt in the heart...

but known
       in
         the
            b o n e s.

-In the Bones

When the outside of your face
looks like the inside of a
g
   r
      a
        v
          e,
everyone so quickly turns a w a y.

Nobody wants to gaze too long upon
the nakedness of pain.

R a r e   is the one
who looks squarely at you,
meets your burning, haunted eyes,
and   s t a y s.

                 -Rare is the One

I will always be grateful to you
for coming into my life
and waking me up.

You are what it feels like
to watch the final slivers of sun
fall and die into the silver ocean,
tangerine, melting sky
giving way to twilight.

-Love & Dusk

You move my nuclei
in an atomic   d   e
                a   c
                n
as I chase the matter of you,
vibrational frequency humming
in motion with our bodies.

We fit into slivers of moonlight
spilling wantonly from windows,
illuminating wolven eyes.
We burn the midnight oil
in the form of sweat and toil

that sticks us into something   n
                                e
                              w.

                    -Object Permanence

I cannot imagine anything else
as tempting as the flames that erupt
when I kiss your skin
and pull you as close to me
as this earthly body will allow.

You taught me
that firestorm love is alchemy,
the purest

                                                                    n.

                                                          o
                                                i
                                    s
                            n
                        e
                  c
            s
a

What better gift is there
than to have your eyes   o p e n e d?

                    -The Alchemy of Fire

I have never seen more clearly:
you, in front of me...
and there is my undoing,
my enlightenment,
my trial by fire,
my turn in the arena.

You will turn me inside out,
and I will let you.

Ruin me, my careless love;
I don't care, just take me home.
Darling, it's so sad but true,
I'm better when I'm
mad
      for
           y o u.

           -Madness

My bones cry out for you.
They've never known your touch,
but they have felt your love...
isn't that   e n o u g h?

You're afraid of forgetting
the feel of my skin against your teeth.
You know *exactly what you're missing*
when you can't   d e v o u r   me.

-Rabid

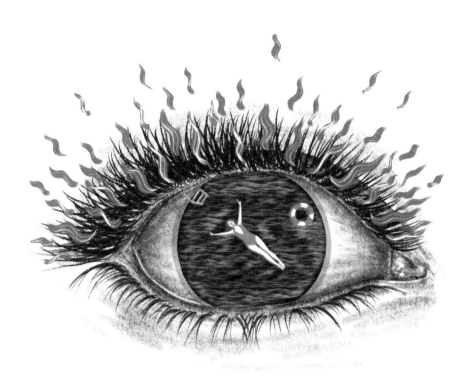

I drank starlight from your lips
as I drowned inside your eyes.

I hung my life upon your fingertips,
as I promised you my life.

I slipped into you,
and I never want to let go.

-Falling Star

If I must pick my poison,
If I am to choose what I am haunted by,

may it always be the heat of those eyes.

One touch, and I combust,
magic fingers yield my skin,
marking every evening I would have sworn
heaven is a place gated by your lips
and hidden upon your tongue.

You
        kiss
                your
                        way
                                s o u t h,
and I find God in your mouth.

                    -Spontaneous Combustion

The newness is gone,
and the butterflies have long since died,
but they've been replaced by *something better.*

I remember when you were still a stranger,
candle on the dresser, and I was shaking;
nervous and dying to touch your skin.

That was so long ago,
and though we are so far from new,
we have aged into something better:

into   "h o m e".

You come in the door;
the day melts off of my shoulders,
and I melt into your arms.

                    -Something Better

I hid,
learned-indifference
encased in walls of stone.
You could have crashed through,
but you refused to break them down.

You instead dismantled them,
brick by brick, one by one,
with eyes so kind,
with soul so gentle,
with heart so strong,
with hands so careful:

such a soft and patient way
to meet me where I was.

I watched you,
The first who ever understood.

You took me by the hand,
And took you by your love.

We are candle glow,
and yellow sun, and golden.

                    -Fallen Fortress

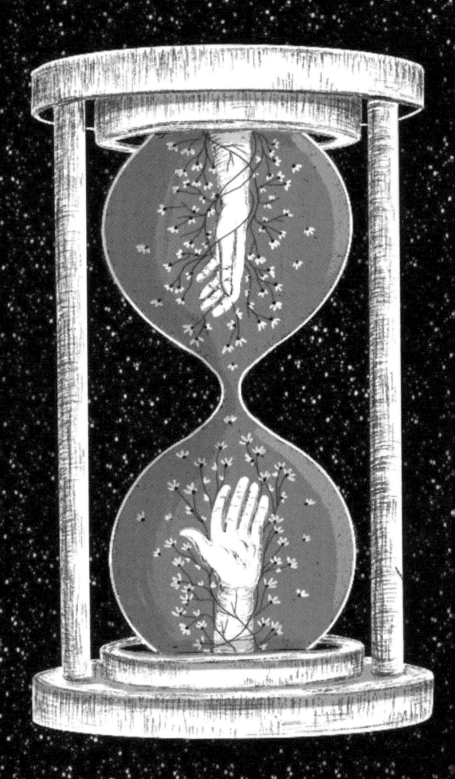

You and I bloom in darkness,
and breathe out sweet magic
with each

                        e
            s
        i
r
and
f
        a
            l
                l
                        of our chests:
hand to hand, and breath to breath.

Steady hums and   s h a r e d   rhythms
find embers in the fire
of dead things we lost to others

but found again in one another.

                    -Lost & Found

The baby steps I took toward you
soon became a landslide.

The fuse you lit within me
soon became a   w i l d f i r e.

You have this beautiful way of
elevating everything.

-Higher Elevation

You are "it" for me.

Once you find this,
you have everything,
and there is no going back
to "ordinary".

"You're so lucky."

That's what I often hear others say
about the love I share with you.

It's not true, and luck has nothing to do with it.

The truth is that we have worked hard
to choose one another every day,
to weather the storms,
to stay when it was hard,
to stoke the fire when we feared it was dead,
and to refuse to give up on us.

We put in the work and the effort.
We fought for our love.
Our "luck" is just us looking
at the stone fortress we built,
and saying, "It is enough".

Our love has always provided a liminal home,
half floating between myth and realm,
and half planted firmly upon the earth.

We fly, we fall, we rise, we burn.

We are wanderers, explorers of the deep,
peeking around the silent corners
that we fear showing to one another.

We are friend and foe, protector and lover.

We cling like breath of life.
We do not fear the night,
or the dawn,
or whatever may come.

We beseech Time to be kind,
and as it continues to move along,
You and I...

we hope, and we l o v e.

-You and I

You and I, evermore.

Let winter come; let the cold settle in our bones.
Let the summer sun burn us half to death.
Let the extremes steal our breath;
we can weather it all.

We always have.

We always will.

Journal Pages

The following is journal
space for you to use as you
see fit.

Think, feel, breathe, and
create something.

Acknowledgments

JMG: Above all else, thank you to my partner in both love and life. Your love, friendship, and endless support make me believe that I am boundless. I will always burn for you.

Avalon: My daughter, my legacy; you are the main reason I get up and breathe each day. I love you more than life.

To my parents: One of you is gone, and one of you still lives. Thank you for giving me life and a legacy of love to pass on.

To my tribe: Thank you for loving me in spite of myself, for exactly who I am.

To Peppermint Lines and Kalyani Datta: You two have blessed me beyond belief in agreeing to be a part of this project. Writers so rarely ever create in a vacuum, so thank you for helping me bring this book to stunning life. You are tremendous artists AND the loveliest humans!

To Kristen, my copy editor and friend: Thank you for being the set of eyes I needed to ensure this book was everything I wanted it to be. You're way better at this than I am!

To my readers: You have changed my life, and I am forever grateful for each and every one of you. Thank you for allowing my words into your hearts.

About the Author

Stefanie Briar is an LGBTQ+ poet, lyricist, educator, and freelance editor best known for the bestselling poetry collection you hold in your hands, *Burn.*

She is a Potterhead and Swiftie who enjoys candles, cancelled plans, and witchy shit. She lives for great music and the power of telling a good story.

She shares her New Jersey home with her husband, daughter, cat, and python.

Connect with her:

@stefanie.briar.poetry

@stefaniebriarpoetry

Other titles by Stefanie Briar:

Cosmosis
Homecoming
Shades of Ruin

"She's mad, but she's magic.
There's no lie in her fire."

-Charles Bukowski

Burn on, human flames.

With love and fire,

S.B.

Printed in Great Britain
by Amazon